Do You Listen?/ ¿Escuchas?

by/por **Joanne Mattern**

Reading consultant/Consultora de lectura: Susan Nations, M.Ed., author/literacy coach/ consultant in literacy development/autora/tutora de alfabetización/ consultora de desarrollo de la lectura

WEEKLY READER® PUBLISHING

Please visit our web site at: www.garethstevens.com
For a free color catalog describing our list of high-quality books,
call 1-800-542-2595 (USA) or 1-800-387-3178 (Canada).

Library of Congress Cataloging-in-Publication Data

Mattern, Joanne, 1963-
 [Do you listen? Spanish & English]
 Do you listen? = ¿Escuchas? / Joanne Mattern.
  p. cm. — (Are you a good friend? = Buenos amigos)
 Includes bibliographical references and index.
 ISBN-10: 0-8368-8284-9 (lib. bdg.)
 ISBN-13: 978-0-8368-8284-1 (lib. bdg.)
 ISBN-10: 0-8368-8289-X (softcover)
 ISBN-13: 978-0-8368-8289-6 (softcover)
  1. Listening—Juvenile literature. 2. Friendship—Juvenile literature.
 I. Title. II. Title: Escuchas?
 BF323.L5M3618   2008
 153.6'8—dc22   2007017355

First published in 2008 by
Weekly Reader® Books
An imprint of Gareth Stevens Publishing
1 Reader's Digest Road
Pleasantville, NY 10570-7000 USA

Copyright © 2008 by Gareth Stevens, Inc.

Editor: Gini Holland
Art direction: Tammy West
Graphic designer: Dave Kowalski
Picture research: Diane Laska-Swanke
Photographer: Gregg Andersen
Production: Jessica Yanke
Spanish translation: Tatiana Acosta and Guillermo Gutiérrez

Printed in the United States of America

1 2 3 4 5 6 7 8 9 11 10 09 08 07

Note to Educators and Parents

Reading is such an exciting adventure for young children! They are beginning to integrate their oral language skills with written language. To encourage children along the path to early literacy, books must be colorful, engaging, and interesting; they should invite the young reader to explore both the print and the pictures.

The *Are You a Good Friend?* series is designed to help children learn the special social skills they need to make and keep friends in their homes, schools, and communities. The books in this series teach the social skills of listening, sharing, helping others, and taking turns, showing readers how and why these skills help establish and maintain good friendships.

Each book is specially designed to support the young reader in the reading process. The familiar topics are appealing to young children and invite them to read — and reread — again and again. The full-color photographs and enhanced text further support the student during the reading process.

In addition to serving as wonderful picture books in schools, libraries, homes, and other places where children learn to love reading, these books are specifically intended to be read within an instructional guided reading group. This small group setting allows beginning readers to work with a fluent adult model as they make meaning from the text. After children develop fluency with the text and content, the books can be read independently. Children and adults alike will find these books supportive, engaging, and fun!

— Susan Nations, M.Ed., author, literacy coach,
and consultant in literacy development

Nota para los maestros y los padres

¡Leer es una aventura tan emocionante para los niños pequeños! A esta edad están comenzando a integrar su manejo del lenguaje oral con el lenguaje escrito. Para animar a los niños en el camino de la lectura incipiente, los libros deben ser coloridos, estimulantes e interesantes; deben invitar a los jóvenes lectores a explorar la letra impresa y las ilustraciones.

Buenos amigos es una colección diseñada para ayudar a los jóvenes lectores a aprender las destrezas sociales necesarias para hacer y mantener amistades en casa, en la escuela y en la comunidad. Mediante los libros de esta colección, los lectores aprenderán por qué escuchar, compartir, turnarse con los demás y brindar ayuda son destrezas sociales necesarias para establecer y mantener buenas amistades.

Cada libro está especialmente diseñado para ayudar a los jóvenes lectores en el proceso de lectura. Los temas familiares llaman la atención de los niños y los invitan a leer una y otra vez. Las fotografías a todo color y el tamaño de la letra ayudan aún más al estudiante en el proceso de lectura.

Además de servir como maravillosos libros ilustrados en escuelas, bibliotecas, hogares y otros lugares donde los niños aprenden a amar la lectura, estos libros han sido especialmente concebidos para ser leídos en un grupo de lectura guiada. Este contexto permite que los lectores incipientes trabajen con un adulto que domina la lectura mientras van determinando el significado del texto. Una vez que los niños dominan el texto y el contenido, los libros pueden ser leídos de manera independiente. ¡Estos libros les resultarán útiles, estimulantes y divertidos a niños y a adultos por igual!

— Susan Nations, M.Ed., autora/tutora de alfabetización/
consultora de desarrollo de la lectura

Are you a good friend? One way to be a good friend is to **listen**. Do you know how to listen?

- - - - - - - - - - - - - - - - - - - -

¿Eres un buen amigo o una buena amiga? Algo que hacen los buenos amigos es **escuchar**. ¿Sabes cómo escuchar?

4

Listening is more than **hearing**. Listening also means thinking about what you are hearing. There are many ways to listen to a friend.

- - - - - - - - - - - - - - - - - - -

Escuchar no es simplemente **oír**. Escuchar significa también pensar en lo que estamos oyendo. Hay muchas maneras de escuchar a los amigos.

You can listen to a friend read
a story. Listening can be fun.

- - - - - - - - - - - - - - - - - - -

Puedes escuchar a tus amigos
cuando leen un cuento. Escuchar
puede ser entretenido.

You can listen to a friend tell a joke.
Listening can be funny!

- - - - - - - - - - - - - - - - - - - -

Puedes escuchar a tus amigos
cuando cuentan un chiste.
¡Escuchar puede ser divertido!

If a friend needs help, you can listen to him. Listening lets you know what to do.

- -

Si un amigo necesita ayuda, lo puedes escuchar. Si lo escuchas, sabrás qué debes hacer.

Sometimes a friend is sad. You
can listen to him share his **feelings**.

A veces, un amigo se siente triste.
Puedes escucharlo cuando habla
de sus **sentimientos**.

14

15

Look at people when they talk.
Looking shows you are listening.

Mira a las personas cuando hablan.
Al mirarlos, demuestras que estás
escuchando.

Wait to speak until your friend is done talking. You cannot talk and listen at the same time!

- - - - - - - - - - - - - - - - - - -

Antes de hablar, espera a que la otra persona haya terminado. ¡No es posible hablar y escuchar al mismo tiempo!

Listening shows that you **care** about your friend. Listening helps you be a good friend.

- - - - - - - - - - - - - - - - - - - -

Escuchar es una forma de demostrar a tus amigos que los **aprecias**. Escuchar nos ayuda a ser buenos amigos.

Glossary

care — to like and want to help someone

feelings — emotions, including happiness, sadness, anger, hope, and fear

hearing — taking in sounds through the ears

listen — to think about what people are saying while they are talking

Glosario

apreciar — sentir afecto por alguien y querer ayudarlo

escuchar — pensar en lo que dicen las personas mientras hablan

oír — captar sonidos por los oídos

sentimientos — emociones como alegría, tristeza, rabia, entusiasmo y miedo

For More Information/ Más información

How to Be a Friend. Laurie Krasny Brown (Little, Brown Young Readers)

Listen and Learn. Learning to Get Along (series). Cheri J. Meiners (Free Spirit Publishing)

We Can Listen. You and Me (series). Denise M. Jordan (Heinemann Library)

Why Should I Listen? Claire Llewellyn (Barron's Educational)

Index

Índice

About the Author

Joanne Mattern has written more than 150 books for children. Joanne also works in her local library. She lives in New York State with her husband, three daughters, and assorted pets. She enjoys animals, music, reading, going to baseball games, and visiting schools to talk about her books.

Información sobre la autora

Joanne Mattern ha escrito más de 150 libros para niños. Además, Joanne trabaja en la biblioteca de su comunidad. Vive en el estado de Nueva York con su esposo, sus tres hijas y varias mascotas. A Joanne le gustan los animales, la música, ir al béisbol, leer y hacer visitas a las escuelas para hablar de sus libros.